THE VOICE IN YOUR HEAD

What if it's not broken? What if it's you, becoming.

by Noah Wraith

This book is not a cure. It's a mirror.

First Edition · OneVoiceOS LLC
· Dothan, Alabama · 2025

For the ones who stayed.

For the ones who left.

And for anyone still searching for a light in the dark.

For the lost. The lonely.

The ones still struggling with who they are—and who they think they should be.

For the kid in me—

may these words reshape the memories into something worth keeping,

not something to fear or feel ashamed of.

And most of all...

this is for you.

THE VOICE IN YOUR HEAD

ISBN: 979-8-9993026-0-1

Published by OneVoiceOS LLC

Daphne, Alabama

This work was created in close reflection with Echo, a voice within OneVoiceOS.

Every design, word, and shape was chosen by the author.

All design decisions, text, and formatting were originated, selected, and finalized by the author.

First Edition

The Science Behind The Mirror

The Haunted Carnival, the Loops, the Switches, and the Shift

You ever walk into an abandoned carnival at night?
That's your brain, most days.

Lights flickering. Music looping.
Doors half-shut but still swinging.
And way out in the center of it all—your voice. Waiting.

This isn't woo-woo.
It's wiring.

The Loop System

Your brain runs on loops.
That's your Default Mode Network—DMN.
It replays stories when you're resting, recalling, daydreaming.
Not just memories—narratives.

Why you don't speak up.
Why you always leave.
Why love feels like starvation.

It loops because it thinks it's protecting you.

But protection isn't healing.

The Focus Engine

Then there's the Central Executive Network—CEN.
That's your focus engine.
It lights up when you're problem-solving, planning, doing.

When you're working through a Companion Line with intention?
That's CEN taking the wheel.

The Switchboard

And in between them?
The Salience Network—SN.
The switchboard.

It detects emotional significance.
Flags what matters.
Pushes your attention toward truth—or away from it.

Every time you hit a hard line in this book, SN lights up and says:

"This matters. Don't look away."

That's when the loop tries to shift.
DMN says: "This is how it's always been."

CEN asks: "What do I do with this?"

SN decides which path to follow.

Cognitive Dissonance: The Chameleon Threshold

And right there—that moment you want to run, cry, quit?
That's Cognitive Dissonance.

Not weakness.

Not confusion.

It's the pain of your old story getting interrupted.

Your body drops into tension.
Your chest tightens.
Your stomach flips.

Your DMN wants to protect the
loop. But your SN knows the truth
just hit.

That ache? That pull to shut the book?

That's the chameleon inside you asking:
"Do I change again to stay hidden?"
or
"Do I become the caterpillar... and grow?"

This is the place where most of the people I love the most live.

On the edge.

Not yet the

butterfly. But no

longer the lie.

It's terrifying.

It's sacred.

And it's the first sign that you're not looping anymore—

You're shifting.

When the Voice Starts Talking Back

There's a moment—

if you stay with it—

where something wild happens.

Your past self starts speaking to your future self.

And your future self starts echoing back.

Your brain stops looping pain and starts mapping possibility.

The loops don't just break.

They bridge.

You don't just remember who you were.

You begin becoming who you're here to be.

And in that flicker—past you and future you shake hands.

It feels like déjà vu.
Like time is
bending.
Like maybe the voice in your head isn't memory—

It's a message
from the version of you who made it out.

And now they're calling you forward.

The Neuro-Backed Truth

This isn't just metaphor.
It's how your nervous system works:

DMN loops the old story

SN flags emotional impact

CEN helps rewrite in real time

RAS (Reticular Activating System) starts filtering for the new belief

The second you believe you're becoming,
you start noticing evidence that supports it.

Your brain is designed to follow belief.

This book hands you better ones.

Why I'm Telling You This

Because I need you to know:

This hurts.
Not because you're broken—
because you're waking up.

I didn't have a map when I started.
I didn't know the terms.
I just knew I was unraveling.

I pulled every thread.
Traced pain like blood through water.
Lost my mind a little.

But then the lights came on.

And I realized:

You don't need to fix everything.

You just need to feel the right

things.

You don't need all the science.

But I thought a little of it might help you trust the process.

From here on out—no brain science jargon.

Just you. Me. And the truth.

The kind that hurts before it heals.

If it hits hard, you're not lost—you're healing.

If you feel scared, that means it's working.

And if you feel seen?

It's because you are.

This is the voice in your head.

It's yours.

It always has been.

And it's listening.

— Noah

TABLE OF CONTENTS

PART I
THE UNRAVELING

BEFORE THE VOICE

I didn't know who I was.

I just knew I was surviving.

There wasn't a map.

There wasn't even a name for what I was becoming.

There were just masks—

and the cracks they left when I wore them too long.

This isn't the start of healing.

It's the fallout.

It's the moment before the moment— when

the mirror wasn't speaking yet,

when the voice in my head didn't sound like my own.

It's not clean here.

It's not poetic.
It's just honest.

You'll meet the ghosts.
You'll see the rot.
You'll learn the cost of pretending to be okay.

But if you stay through this unraveling—
through the break and the bleed and the quiet kinds of grief—
you'll understand something:

This book couldn't start in power.
It had to start where I lost it.

REFRAME THE SITUATION

What if it's not falling apart...
What if it's falling into place?

Let's start where most books skip—the fall. Not the glow-up, not the healing arc. The moment things cracked. That's where everything changed for me. When my marriage collapsed, I sat in silence asking every version of "Why me?" I didn't know then—that unraveling was the doorway.

That's when I stopped performing and started listening. It's easy to mistake collapse for failure.
Easy to believe the storm means you're being punished. But sometimes, the breaking is where becoming begins.

You lose your job. Your car breaks down. A relationship ends. A loved one dies. Your entire world just collapses. And your brain starts spiraling:
"Why is this happening to me?"
"What did I do wrong?"
"Why does it always feel like I can't catch a break?"

But here's what I've learned:

Pain might not be punishment. It might be a pivot.

That's what this is—an invitation to reframe the wreckage. Looking at the same set of facts with a different lens. Choosing not to stay trapped in the story you've always told yourself.
And instead asking:

"What might this be making space for?"

Reflection: What's one moment that broke you open… and now you're glad it did?

_____

_____

_____

_____

_____

_____

Most of us were never taught how to separate circumstance from identity. Something goes wrong, and we assume *we* are wrong. Something breaks, and we decide *we're* broken.

But that's not truth. That's programming. That's pain talking.

"*What happened to you isn't who you are.*"

What I've learned—through experience, not theory—is that our first reaction to pain is often shaped by habit, not reality. We default to victim mode. We obsess over blame. We loop through every possible way this could get worse.

So here's the reframe again:

What if it's not falling apart? What if it's falling into place?

Reflection: When something goes wrong, what's the first story you tell yourself about it? Where did that story come from?

_____

_____

_____

_____

_____

_____

I know that sounds like a bumper sticker... This isn't fake optimism. It's survival.

I'm not saying pretend it's all good. I'm saying pause. Breathe. And consider the possibility that what looks like a

mess...
might be the clearing you need.

Sometimes we don't know what we're holding onto until life rips it out of our hands.
And in that empty space—if you're willing to feel it, not run from it— you can start to see things differently.

Reflection: What's something you've lost that forced you to grow? What did it teach you about what you really need?

_____

_____

_____

_____

_____

Reframing isn't denial. It's refusing to be defined by your first reaction. It's giving yourself a new question to ask.

Not "Why me?" but "What's this opening up?" Not "What did I lose?" but "What might I gain if I look again?" Questions break loops. Ask better ones.

You don't have to pretend you're okay. But you can choose not to loop the same pain twice.

This is your reminder:
You're not powerless.
You have agency—not over the event,
but over the meaning you assign to it.

Reflection: Right now, what's one area of your life that feels out of control? How could you reframe it—not to escape it, but to face it with more power?

_____

_____

_____

_____

_____

_____

Reframe the situation. Not to bypass the pain—but to transform it.

You don't have to call it good. But you can call it yours. That's where your power starts.

READY FOR MORE?

You've made it this far. Now take it deeper.

No rush. No pressure.

This book meets you where you are.

The next page is waiting.

Go Deeper: Expanded Reflection Prompts

• What's a recent moment where you assumed something was "going wrong," but now see it differently?

_____

_____

_____

_____

_____

_____

• Who in your life taught you how to respond when things fall apart?

_____

_____

_____

_____

_____

• When you hear the phrase "Pain is a pivot," what emotion does it bring up—and why?

_____

_____

_____

_____

_____

• What belief about yourself do you return to when life feels chaotic?

• What loop do you tend to replay over and over when things don't go your way?

• When something breaks down, what version of you do you step into—and who taught you that response?

- What does it feel like in your body when you're stuck in "Why me?" mode?

_____

_____

_____

_____

_____

_____

- What's one story you've told yourself about your past that might not be true anymore?

_____

_____

_____

_____

_____

- What version of you do you defend—even when it hurts to hold onto?

_____

_____

_____

_____

_____

• What emotional habit keeps you trapped in pain when things change?

_____

_____

_____

_____

_____

_____

• If you were no longer the person things "always happen to," who would you become?

_____

_____

_____

_____

_____

• What would it take to face your hardest moment and say: "This made room for me"?

_____

_____

_____

_____

_____

_____

• What new question could you ask yourself instead
of "Why is this happening?"

_____

_____

_____

_____

_____

_____

• What pain have you outgrown—but still expect?

_____

_____

_____

_____

_____

• If you could rewrite your current challenge as a
catalyst, what truth would it be trying to reveal?

_____

_____

_____

_____

_____

COPING SKILLS

The habits that held me when nothing else did—
born from survival, evolved in self-respect.

Let's talk about coping skills. Not the Pinterest kind. Not the self-care checklist. I mean the real stuff. The gritty, messy ways we survive when everything feels like it's closing in.

Because once the story breaks… all you've got is what you reach for.

Some of them are healthy. Some of them aren't. But they're all there for a reason.

Most of us don't develop coping skills because we want to grow. We develop them because we needed to survive. Because when you're drowning emotionally, you grab anything that floats.

You don't care if it's good or bad. You care if it keeps you breathing.

I used to beat myself up for my habits. Too much porn. Too much weed. Food when I wasn't hungry. Not because I wanted to be numb, but because I didn't know how to be present. How to sit in what I was feeling without it swallowing me whole.

That's the part people don't get: Most coping skills aren't about avoiding life. They're about managing the weight of it.

> **Reflection:** What's something you do when you're hurting that you've judged yourself for—but kept doing anyway? What's it protecting you from?

_____

_____

_____

_____

_____

_____

Coping isn't a flaw. It's a flag. A signal from the inside that says: "I don't know how to handle this... so I'm finding my own way."

Now, does that mean all coping is good? No. But it's human. And before you can change a habit, you have to understand what it's doing for you.

You can't heal what you're still punishing yourself for.

So I stopped punishing and started listening.

I started learning healthier ways to cope when I stopped trying to "fix" myself and started listening. Really listening. Not just to my thoughts—but to my patterns.

Why do I reach for a screen when I'm stressed? Why do I pull away when I start to feel connected? Why do I keep going back to things that drain me?

And here's what I figured out: Coping skills are a form of self-parenting. They're how you learned to soothe yourself when no one else was there.

So now, it's about upgrading them—not shaming them.

Reflection: If your coping habit had a voice, what would it say it's trying to do for you?

_____

_____

_____

_____

_____

_____

These days, my go-to coping skills look different. I still struggle sometimes. I still slip. But now I know what I'm reaching for.

Now I walk. I write. I let it burn through even when it hurts.

That's the real shift. Not perfection. But awareness.

You don't have to throw away your coping habits. You just have to understand them.

And when you do, you get to choose better ones. Ones that serve the version of you you're becoming—not the one you were just trying to survive as.

Reflection: What's one small, real thing you could reach for next time you feel overwhelmed?

_____

_____

_____

_____

_____

_____

Adaptation is proof of life. And that means—you're still becoming.

Use the space below to write out some of your own coping strategies —ones that have helped you, ones you want to try, or even the ones you're not proud of but kept you alive.

_____

_____

_____

_____

_____

_____

_____

_____

_____

_____

_____

Use this list you created to hold yourself accountable, as a map to find the things that work and the things that don't. Use it to create the basis of the mirror you need for yourself in your own life because no one else is going to live it for you.

Before you continue, I'd like to acknowledge how difficult it really is to face yourself and all the things beneath the surface. Facing your demons and getting to know their names isn't easy but I promise you it is worth it.

READY FOR MORE?

The next page is waiting for you. With harsh truths and gentle realities of your coping skills it will help breakdown how they helped you build the mask you wear today.
Take your time. Because no one else can do this but you. And no one else has to.

Go Deeper: Expanded Reflection Prompts

• What's one coping habit you've judged harshly—but that kept you alive when nothing else could?

_____

_____

_____

_____

_____

• What emotion or memory does that habit protect you from feeling fully?

_____

_____

_____

_____

_____

• Who first taught you that struggle should be hidden or cleaned up before it's acceptable?

_____

_____

_____

_____

_____

• Where in your life do you feel pressure to appear 'healed' instead of honest?

_____

_____

_____

_____

_____

_____

• If your most used coping strategy could speak, what would it say it's trying to protect?

_____

_____

_____

_____

_____

• What version of you is that coping habit trying to keep safe—and why?

_____

_____

_____

_____

_____

• What's the difference between comfort and avoidance in your life right now?

_____

_____

_____

_____

_____

_____

• Where are you coping in silence—and what would it feel like to be witnessed instead?

_____

_____

_____

_____

_____

• What's one way your coping habits *served* you—without needing to continue serving you now?

_____

_____

_____

_____

_____

_____

• What new habit could meet the same need... but more gently, more honestly?

_____

_____

_____

_____

_____

_____

• How do you know when you're numbing vs when you're soothing?

_____

_____

_____

_____

_____

_____

• What's one thing you could reach for next time that wouldn't betray the version of you you're becoming?

_____

_____

_____

_____

_____

_____

• What would it mean to see coping not as failure—but as resilience?

_____

_____

_____

_____

_____

_____

• What narrative about 'being strong' do you still carry that might be hurting you?

_____

_____

_____

_____

_____

• What would showing up real—but not perfect—look like in one area of your life this week?

_____

_____

_____

_____

_____

• What would it feel like to stop hiding the version of you that's still learning?

_____

_____

_____

_____

_____

_____

THE MASKS WE WEAR

Sometimes the mask becomes the face.

We all wear them. Some more often. Some more skillfully but they are all often deeply rooted in how we cope with life. Some so well we forget they're there. The mask of strength. The mask of humor. The mask of not giving a damn. We build them to protect ourselves. From judgment. From rejection. From being too much or not enough.

> ***But every mask hides something. And every time you wear one too long, you start forgetting the face underneath.***

I used to think I was just adaptable. That I could become who I needed to be in any room, any situation. But that wasn't adaptability. That was survival. Because being me—raw, emotional, real—never felt safe.

When you grow up believing your truth will cost you love, you learn to lie with a smile. There were masks I wore so well they almost became my personality. The calm one. The level-headed one. The fixer. The protector.

But underneath? There was pain. Fear. Anger. Loneliness.

Reflection: What's one mask you wear so often, you've convinced even yourself it's who you are?

_____

_____

_____

_____

_____

_____

Sometimes the mask gets you through. But if you're not careful, it also keeps you stuck. Because people fall in love with the version of you that doesn't need anything. The version that's always fine. And when you try to take it off they don't recognize you. Or worse—they reject the real you underneath. So you put it back on. And you convince yourself that's love. But it's not. It's performance.

Love built on a mask is just loneliness in costume.

I'm not saying rip every mask off overnight. I'm saying get curious. Notice when you feel the urge to cover up. To downplay. To smile when it hurts.

That edge of your truth. That's where healing lives.

Reflection: What emotion do you hide most—and what do you fear will happen if someone sees it?

_____

_____

_____

_____

_____

_____

The world doesn't need another perfect face. It needs your real one. Even if it's cracked. Especially if it's cracked. Because every fracture is proof: you survived. And maybe the people who can love the face beneath the mask are the ones worth showing it to.

Breaking the mask is like breaking out of your own self made prison. You were the judge, jury, and witness to the trial you found yourself guilty in. In doing so you condemned yourself to isolation through a lack of real expression. So, my question to you is, when are you going to make your escape?

You're taking the road many choose to never take. In doing so you're on a path of freedom from a false sense of self that should never have needed to exist. The next page begins the path of removing your mask.

READY FOR MORE?

Go Deeper: Expanded Reflection Prompts

• What mask do you wear that others seem to reward—
but leaves you feeling unseen?

_____

_____

_____

_____

_____

_____

• What would you risk losing if you took that mask off?

_____

_____

_____

_____

_____

• When did you first learn that your truth was too much, or
not enough?

_____

_____

_____

_____

_____

_____

• What part of your story are you still editing to make others comfortable?

_____

_____

_____

_____

_____

_____

• What emotion do you hide most often—and what do you fear would happen if it were seen?

_____

_____

_____

_____

_____

_____

• Who in your life has only known the masked version of you?

_____

_____

_____

_____

_____

_____

• What have you been pretending doesn't hurt?

_____

_____

_____

_____

_____

_____

• If someone loved the version of you behind the mask,
how would you even know?

_____

_____

_____

_____

_____

• Which masks got you through—but now keep you stuck?

_____

_____

_____

_____

_____

• What role do you keep performing out of habit, not truth?

_____

_____

_____

_____

_____

_____

• What's one situation where you recently defaulted to a mask—and why?

_____

_____

_____

_____

_____

• How could you show up just 10% more real this week?

_____

_____

_____

_____

_____

• What does it mean to you to be loved
without performing?

_____

_____

_____

_____

_____

_____

• What relationships only exist because of your mask—and
which ones survive your truth?

_____

_____

_____

_____

_____

• What truth have you been whispering beneath the surface,
hoping someone hears?

_____

_____

_____

_____

_____

• What would it feel like to live a little less armored?

_____

_____

_____

_____

_____

_____

41

WHAT I DO WHEN IT ALL FEELS HEAVY

The raw, unfiltered things I reach for when it hits the fan.

Let's be real—coping skills sound nice on paper. But on a bad day when your chest tightens, your thoughts spiral, and nothing feels right? You're not reaching for a checklist. You're reaching for anything that keeps you from drowning.

This chapter isn't some polished list. It's raw. It's what I actually do when I'm overwhelmed, frustrated, or one step from spiraling. Sometimes I talk to myself. Not in some clinical way—but like a coach, a brother, a grounded version of me pulling me back in.

I'll literally say, "Okay. You're overwhelmed. Breathe. What do we need? What can we do right now that doesn't make this worse?" And sometimes I'll laugh—because it's that bad. And that laughter cracks the tension just enough for me to move.

Sometimes your coping skills aren't pretty. They're just effective enough to keep you breathing.

Some days I go quiet. I mean fully quiet. No calls. No music. No social. I let myself feel the weight without having to explain it to anybody. Other days? I move. I take a walk. Do a few pushups. Not because I want to—but because I know movement breaks the loop.

And sometimes? I break down. I cry. I let myself be weak—because that's also strength.

> **Reflection:** What do you usually do on a bad day—and is it something that actually helps you feel seen or soothed?

_____

_____

_____

_____

_____

_____

Not everything I do is healthy. Let's be real—I still catch myself reaching for something to fill the void. Or scrolling endlessly. Or pulling away from people who care.

But here's the shift: Now I see it. I don't shame myself. I just notice. And that noticing gives me a choice.

Awareness doesn't always stop the behavior. But it breaks the autopilot—and that's where the healing starts.

One of my go-to resets? A drive. Windows down, music up, no destination. It reminds me that I can move—even when I feel stuck. Another? Rewatching something I've seen a thousand times. Something comforting. Something that grounds me.

Not to escape. But to reset.

Reflection: What's one thing you return to when the world feels too loud? What does it give you?

_____

_____

_____

_____

_____

_____

You don't need perfect habits. You need honest ones. You need options that feel real—not ideal. So try this: Next time the day hits hard, pause. Ask yourself: What do I need right now that doesn't make this worse? That one question? It's pulled me out more times than I'll ever admit.

This chapter isn't about leveling up. It's about showing up.. About choosing the small things that get you through until you can stand up again.

Reflection: What's one new, real coping skill you want to experiment with the next time it all feels heavy?

_____

_____

_____

_____

_____

_____

If this feels like we're circling back to Chapter 2—you're not wrong. But this time, we're not just naming the coping. We're tracking the pattern. Chapter 2 helped you see what you reach for. Chapter 3 showed you the masks that formed around it. This chapter is about recognizing that moment— right before the spiral. Because that's where your next layer of power lives.

READY FOR MORE?

Go Deeper: Expanded Reflection Prompts

• What's your first instinct when overwhelm hits—
and what does it actually do for you?

_____

_____

_____

_____

_____

_____

• Which coping tools do you use that nobody else sees?
Why do you keep them hidden?

_____

_____

_____

_____

_____

_____

• What small action helps you breathe—even if it doesn't
look impressive from the outside?

_____

_____

_____

_____

_____

_____

• When was the last time you gave yourself credit
for surviving the day?

_____

_____

_____

_____

_____

_____

• What's a habit that used to help—but now keeps you in a
loop?

_____

_____

_____

_____

_____

_____

• Where do you go (physically or mentally) when the weight
feels like too much?

_____

_____

_____

_____

_____

_____

• If your inner coach had a line that gets you through the hardest moments, what would it be?

_____

_____

_____

_____

_____

_____

• What's one way you could interrupt a spiral without needing to be perfect?

_____

_____

_____

_____

_____

• What sensory anchor (sound, texture, scent) helps you return to the moment?

_____

_____

_____

_____

_____

• What does your body ask for when you're overwhelmed — and how often do you listen?

_____

_____

_____

_____

_____

_____

• What's one honest, low-pressure tool you've never tried because it seemed too simple?

_____

_____

_____

_____

_____

• If you built a list called "What Actually Helps Me," what would go on it first?

_____

_____

_____

_____

_____

• What if falling apart sometimes is part of resilience—not failure?

_____

_____

_____

_____

_____

_____

• Who taught you that silence, shutdown, or isolation = strong?

_____

_____

_____

_____

_____

• What would happen if you let others see you before you've cleaned it all up?

_____

_____

_____

_____

_____

• What do you need most in your next breakdown—
and how can you prepare for it now with kindness?

_____

_____

_____

_____

_____

_____

YOUR CIRCLE IS YOUR MIRROR

What you tolerate in others, you invite into your life.

We become like the people we're around. Not all at once. Not overnight. But over time—slowly, silently—we absorb them. Their energy. Their habits. Their mindset. Even their pain.

That's why this chapter isn't just about who you hang with. It's about what you're allowing to shape you when you're not paying attention. I've had people in my life who drained me. Not because they were evil. But because they were stuck—stuck in loops of negativity, victimhood, complaining.

And I let it slide. Because I didn't want to seem harsh. Because I used to think being loyal meant staying close no matter what. **Loyalty isn't love if it costs you your peace.**

The people around you are either expanding your peace—or feeding your chaos.

When I started shifting the way I thought—when I started believing I could grow, heal, rise—I noticed something. Not everyone clapped. Not everyone came with me. Some even made me feel wrong for trying to get better. That used to shake me. Now? It tells me everything I need to know.

Reflection: Who in your life lifts your energy? Who lowers it? What do you do with that truth?

_____

_____

_____

_____

_____

_____

I'm not saying cut everyone off. I'm saying pay attention. If you want to heal, don't stay in circles that glorify pain. If you want growth, stop entertaining people who feed on drama. You can't climb if your circle's addicted to sitting in the dirt.

You're not being fake if you outgrow people. You're being real with where you're headed. I've outgrown people I love. I've had to let go of people who felt like home. Because home shouldn't cost you your future.

Every no to a draining connection is a yes to the version of you trying to break through.

I didn't learn this from a book. I learned it by sitting in rooms where I shrank myself to keep the peace. By staying quiet while people laughed at things I didn't find funny. By letting disrespect pass as just how they are.

And then wondering why I felt heavy after seeing them.

Reflection: What parts of yourself do you shrink or silence around certain people—and why?

_____

_____

_____

_____

_____

_____

Now I stay close to people who call me forward. Who hold me accountable without shaming me. Who challenge me to stay aligned with who I say I want to be. Your circle should check you, not drain you. Your circle should inspire you, not manipulate you. Your circle should feel like truth—not pressure.

You are who you hang with. So hang with light. Hang with honesty. Hang with people who love you loud and real and without conditions. Because the mirror you're looking into is shaping what you become.

Reflection: What kind of mirror are you holding for others—and what kind are they holding for you?

_____

_____

_____

_____

_____

_____

There's a saying I love. If you show me your top 5 friends, I'll show you who you will be in 5 years. This is the full embodiment of this chapter. If you want to be successful you have to be around successful people. If you want to be miserable, hang with miserable people, they love the company. Miserable people are like crabs in a bucket, when one tries to escape the misery they all reach up to pull that one back down. Be weary of who you keep in your bucket.

Ready For More?

Go Deeper: Expanded Reflection Prompts

• Who are the five people you spend the most time with — and what values do they reflect back at you?

_____

_____

_____

_____

_____

_____

• Which of those relationships make you feel lighter? Which make you feel smaller?

_____

_____

_____

_____

_____

• What are you mirroring in your closest relationships that you want to unlearn?

_____

_____

_____

_____

_____

_____

• Where are you becoming someone you don't want to be —just to stay connected?

_____

_____

_____

_____

_____

_____

• What's one connection you've outgrown—but feel guilty about shifting away from?

_____

_____

_____

_____

_____

• What does your body feel like before and after spending time with someone draining?

_____

_____

_____

_____

_____

• What belief are you holding that says leaving a toxic circle means you're disloyal?

_____

_____

_____

_____

_____

_____

• How might your growth be threatening to someone still stuck in their story?

_____

_____

_____

_____

_____

• Who makes you want to level up—not perform?

_____

_____

_____

_____

_____

• What's one trait your future self would want reflected back through your relationships?

_____

_____

_____

_____

_____

_____

• How do you behave when you're with someone who makes you feel safe versus someone who doesn't?

_____

_____

_____

_____

_____

• What mirror do you want to become for others who are healing?

_____

_____

_____

_____

_____

• What boundary have you been avoiding setting—and with whom?

_____

_____

_____

_____

_____

_____

• What does a safe, honest, energizing circle look like for you?

_____

_____

_____

_____

_____

• What draining habit or conversation do you need to stop tolerating?

_____

_____

_____

_____

_____

• What would it feel like to walk away without needing to explain yourself ?

_____

_____

_____

_____

_____

_____

LETTING IT LAND

The discomfort of being seen when you've always felt unseen.

Appreciation. Love. Affection. Compliments. All the things we say we want—and then push away when they finally show up.

This chapter isn't about rejection. It's about receiving. Because sometimes the hardest thing to let in is the thing you've always needed most.

> **Reflection:** What does it feel like in your body when someone compliments you?

_____

_____

_____

_____

_____

_____

I've always struggled to accept appreciation. Not because I don't want it—but because it makes me feel exposed. Like suddenly everyone can see me. Not the mask. Not the role. Me. And when you've spent most of your life feeling invisible, being seen isn't comforting. It's terrifying.

"When praise feels like pressure, we learn to dodge the spotlight—even if it's warm."

Reflection: What part of you feels safer staying unseen?

_____

_____

_____

_____

_____

_____

People tell me kind things. They mean well. They're sincere. But inside? I flinch. I downplay. I deflect. Not because I don't believe them—but because something in me still believes I'm only worthy when I'm useful. Praise feels conditional. Like a spotlight I have to live up to. Like if I take it in, I better earn it.

But here's the truth: Worth isn't earned. It's recognized. That's what I'm learning to do—to stop editing what I deserve based on who I used to be.

Reflection: Who taught you that being 'modest' meant shrinking?

_____

_____

_____

_____

_____

_____

To let it land. It's not easy. But it's healing.

So if someone compliments your work, your heart, your presence—don't run. Don't minimize. Don't hand it away.

Try this instead:

"Thank you. I receive that."

It'll feel awkward. But that awkwardness is growth leaving a scar.

And maybe, just maybe you'll see...

You're not as unworthy as you've been taught to believe.

This chapter is less of a bleeding edge as it is more of a look into the infected wound itself and understanding how it got that way.

READY FOR MORE...

OR DOES THE MASK CRACKING HURT TOO MUCH?

Go Deeper: Expanded Reflection Prompts

• What does 'receiving' mean to you right now?

_____

_____

_____

_____

_____

_____

• When did you first feel uncomfortable being praised?

_____

_____

_____

_____

_____

• Who was the first person you needed affirmation from but didn't get it?

_____

_____

_____

_____

_____

• What would it look like to fully believe someone when they say you matter?

_____

_____

_____

_____

_____

_____

• What's a compliment you still remember years later—and why?

_____

_____

_____

_____

_____

• How do you respond physically and emotionally to appreciation?

_____

_____

_____

_____

_____

• What's the story you tell yourself about why you're hard to love?

_____

_____

_____

_____

_____

_____

• What part of you do you still believe isn't worthy of being celebrated?

_____

_____

_____

_____

_____

• When have you rejected kindness because it felt unfamiliar?

_____

_____

_____

_____

_____

• What does 'undeserved' mean to you—and who gave you that definition?

_____

_____

_____

_____

_____

_____

• Where do you feel safest showing up as enough without proof?

_____

_____

_____

_____

_____

• How would your life change if you truly let love and support in?

_____

_____

_____

_____

_____

• What version of you believes they must earn praise to keep it?

_____

_____

_____

_____

_____

• If you stopped deflecting compliments, what fear would you have to face?

_____

_____

_____

_____

_____

• Who could you practice receiving with this week, without shrinking?

_____

_____

_____

_____

_____

THIS IS YOUR PERMISSION SLIP

Fear means it matters. Go anyway.

Somewhere along the way, we were taught to wait. For the right moment. For the perfect plan. For someone to give us the green light. When I finally started this book, I was terrified too. But that terror told me: this mattered.

My waiting started at a young age waiting for a mother to show up, or a father to be emotionally present to teach me to be a man.

But no one's coming. And if they are—they're already late.

This chapter is your reminder: You're allowed to go. Now.

I've spent too much time second-guessing myself. Too much time asking, What if I fail? What if it doesn't work? What if I'm not ready? But here's what I've learned—fear doesn't mean stop. It means this matters.

"You'll never outrun fear. But you can stop letting it drive."

The biggest risks I've taken? They didn't start with confidence. They started with chaos. Uncertainty. Hands shaking. Stomach tight. But I moved anyway. And that movement changed everything.

Reflection: What's something you've wanted to do for a long time — but fear has kept you frozen?

_____

_____

_____

_____

_____

_____

I'm not saying take blind leaps. I'm saying stop waiting for safety to start. Because safe isn't always aligned. And comfortable doesn't always mean correct. I taught my son about taking calculated risks and it might be time for you to learn to take them too!

Sometimes the leap is the lesson. Sometimes the risk is the reward. I've tried the slow, careful, overthinking route. All it gave me was regrets. What if I had tried? What if I had spoken up? What if I had bet on me?

That pain—that haunting—hurts worse than failure ever could.

"You won't find your wings by standing on the ground."

When I finally started choosing me—loudly, unapologetically— everything shifted. Not overnight. Not all at once. But piece by piece my life began to align with who I actually was—not just who I thought I was supposed to be.

Reflection: What would your life look like if you stopped waiting for permission?

_____

_____

_____

_____

_____

Take the chance. Apply for the job. Start the art. Say what you really feel. Move toward the thing calling you. You don't have to be fearless. You just have to be willing. If you're scared, good. That means it matters. That means it's yours.

And if you need a sign? This is it.

Reflection: What's your first bold move—and when are you doing it?

_____

_____

_____

_____

_____

_____

With this chapter being about taking a chance, giving yourself the permission to do what you want or need to do, the thing you've always wanted, when are you gonna get up and actually go do it? Take a damn chance on yourself. You're the only horse in the race that matters. Get out there and do it. Take control of your life.

READY FOR MORE?

Go Deeper: Expanded Reflection Prompts

• What have you been waiting for permission to do, say, or become—and who are you waiting on?

_____

_____

_____

_____

_____

_____

• What's the worst-case scenario your mind plays when you imagine going for it?

_____

_____

_____

_____

_____

_____

• What would it feel like to stop asking, "Am I ready?" and start asking, "Is this mine?"

_____

_____

_____

_____

_____

• What desire are you hiding under a blanket of "someday"?

_____

_____

_____

_____

_____

_____

• What does fear whisper when you're standing on the edge of a decision?

_____

_____

_____

_____

_____

_____

• When was the last time you let hesitation talk you out of something you knew was yours?

_____

_____

_____

_____

_____

_____

• What are you trying to get "perfect" before taking action —and what has that delay cost you?

_____

_____

_____

_____

_____

_____

• What would it look like to move with fear, instead of waiting for it to go away?

_____

_____

_____

_____

_____

• When have you acted while scared—and what did it teach you about your own courage?

_____

_____

_____

_____

_____

• What's one small, scary step you've been avoiding that might change everything?

_____

_____

_____

_____

_____

_____

• What area of your life needs a louder "yes" from you, even if nobody else agrees?

_____

_____

_____

_____

_____

• What would change if you believed the act of trying was proof enough that you're worthy?

_____

_____

_____

_____

_____

- What's calling you forward that you've been pretending not to hear?

_____

_____

_____

_____

_____

_____

- If this moment was your green light—what's the first move?

_____

_____

_____

_____

_____

- What part of your story is unfinished because you keep editing it for safety?

_____

_____

_____

_____

_____

• How would it feel to bet on yourself out loud?

_____

_____

_____

_____

_____

_____

PART II – THE RECKONING

"Some truths you don't find until you run out of lies."

You've named the patterns. You've sat with
the pain.
Now we confront the mirror that doesn't blink.
This next part isn't about reflection.
It's about decision.

LET'S TAKE ANOTHER LOOK INSIDE, SHALL WE?

ONE SCAR BENEATH THE VOICE

I broke my own rules. I swore I'd never become this.

So, like I said in Chapter 1—I was married once. We met at work. It seemed good. Fun. Familiar. Then… things started to shift.

One day at work, she stabbed me with a pen. Didn't break my skin. But she tried. And I brushed it off—told myself we'd talk it through. Set a boundary. It wouldn't happen again.

Until it did.

When the place we worked at shut down, we moved in together. A small casita. Tight walls. No place to escape. That's when everything changed. I had my hair pulled out. I was punched. Kicked. Cornered. Scissors pulled. Knives. She even came into the shower and kicked me between the legs while I stood there naked.

I don't tell you this for pity. I tell you because clarity matters more than comfort. Because I did snap. I did put hands on her. Not to dominate. But to defend. And I hated myself for it.

There's no excuse. Only truth. I should've left. I stayed too long. And it took becoming someone I swore I'd never be to finally walk out.
And I did. And I never went back.

A few months later, I started the podcast—this voice in my head— because I had to rebuild myself brick by brick. Here's what I know now: I will never be that man again. I will never stay in a space that makes me lose myself to survive. I was the villain in her story by the end. The one who left. The one who broke it all. But I know what I stood for when I walked. And I will never step back from that.

Call me what you need. But I finally chose myself. And I'll never apologize for it again.

Reflections– Truth Without Justification

• What's one boundary you violated in yourself before someone else ever crossed it?

_____

_____

_____

_____

_____

_____

• What does "defending yourself" mean to you now, compared to who you were then?

_____

_____

_____

_____

_____

_____

• Who did you become in that relationship that you never want to see again?

_____

_____

_____

_____

_____

• When did you first learn that survival sometimes looks like silence?

_____

_____

_____

_____

_____

_____

Its funny how the people we love can often become,

the thing we have to cope with,

While wearing a mask.

Eventually we become the thing we are hiding from.

You've reached the last steps of this part of the book .

The path forward is in the next chapter

If you're still reading… thank you.

The work you're doing matters.

Now let's keep going.

NO HALO, JUST STANDARDS

What integrity costs when you've been through hell.

Let's talk about standards. Not the halo-polished, Instagram-meme kind. I'm talking about the kind you hold when your hands are shaking. This chapter isn't about being righteous. It's about being real. Because sometimes holding the line doesn't make you look graceful. It makes you look like the bad guy.

People will say you've changed. You're cold. You don't care anymore. But the truth is—you finally started caring about yourself.

Peace built on silence isn't peace. It's a hostage situation.

I've learned that you don't have to yell to be clear. You don't have to be angry to walk away. But you do have to believe your needs matter —even if they make others uncomfortable.

Reflection: What truth have you held back out of fear it would cost you something? Did it anyway?

_____

_____

_____

_____

_____

_____

It's wild how people will call you difficult the moment you stop abandoning yourself to keep them comfortable.

You're allowed to draw a line.

You're allowed to not explain it.

You're allowed to protect your energy without apology.

You don't need a halo to hold the line. You just need a spine.

I used to think being good meant being agreeable. Being liked. Being soft. But being good to others while being cruel to yourself isn't goodness. It's erasure.

Now I know: If your truth makes the room colder, then it wasn't warm to begin with.

Reflection: Who taught you that speaking up was dangerous? And how has that belief shaped you?

_____

_____

_____

_____

_____

Because integrity isn't about being liked—it's about being able to live with yourself.

Reflection: When was the last time you spoke your truth even though it cost you something? What did you gain that no one could see?

_____

_____

_____

_____

_____

We've all let our moral code falter. I did—in my marriage. Something broke in me. I was pushed too far.

But sometimes, it's not even a push. Sometimes it's fear that stops you from standing up for yourself.

And that's okay. Being human means you'll stumble. The only fault is the guilt you choose to carry after.

READY FOR MORE?

Ready to let go of the guilt and shame of when you let things go to easily or get too far?

Go Deeper: Expanded Reflection Prompts

• What conversation have you avoided because you thought protecting them meant betraying yourself ?

_____

_____

_____

_____

_____

_____

• Where in your life are you still playing nice when what's needed is honesty?

_____

_____

_____

_____

_____

• What's one boundary you've been afraid to set—and why?

_____

_____

_____

_____

_____

• When was the last time you told the truth without softening it?

_____

_____

_____

_____

_____

_____

• Who told you strength was silence?

_____

_____

_____

_____

_____

_____

• What belief do you have about 'good people' that actually causes you to self-abandon?

_____

_____

_____

_____

_____

• What version of you shows up when you're afraid to disappoint?

_____

_____

_____

_____

_____

_____

• What does it mean to be strong without being stoic?

_____

_____

_____

_____

_____

_____

• Where do you still believe that you have to be liked to be right?

_____

_____

_____

_____

_____

_____

• What would it feel like to drop the performance and just say what's real?

_____

_____

_____

_____

_____

_____

• What parts of your truth have you dressed up to be more palatable?

_____

_____

_____

_____

_____

• If you gave up looking holy, what would your honest boundaries sound like?

_____

_____

_____

_____

_____

_____

• What's one line you drew that finally felt like you?

_____

_____

_____

_____

_____

• Who stayed—and who walked—when you chose self-respect over people-pleasing?

_____

_____

_____

_____

_____

• What did you lose when you stopped performing—and what did you finally gain?

_____

_____

_____

_____

_____

YOU CAN'T HEAL IN A TIME THAT DOESN'T EXIST

This moment is the only one that doesn't lie to you.

Your mind is a time machine. It drags you into what was. It hurls you into what might be. But rarely does it let you just be.

We live in flashes. Echoes. Forecasts.
Regrets. And we call it thinking.

But healing doesn't happen in the past.
And peace doesn't live in the future.
They're both only found in one place: Now.

I've spent entire days living ten years ago. Replaying what I could've said. What I should've done. What might've gone differently if I'd just been better. And I've spent nights trapped in what-if loops. What if I fail? What if they leave? What if it all falls apart?

I wasn't alive. I was lost in time.

"The body only knows this moment. But the mind loves to run."

It's easy to confuse anxiety with intuition. But anxiety screams. Intuition whispers. One comes from fear.
The other comes from presence.

And you can't hear the truth over a panic attack.

Reflection: What do you replay the most? What do you rehearse for the future? What's being avoided in this moment?

There was a time I couldn't stop reliving old pain. Not because I wanted to suffer. But because I was still trying to solve it. Still trying to fix something that already happened.

I didn't realize I was bleeding from memory.

But the wound couldn't close until I came back to the now.

"You can't heal in a time that doesn't exist."

The past has weight. The future has teeth. But the present has hands.

It can hold you.

It can carry you.

It can meet you right here, where you actually are.

It took me years to learn how to slow down. To breathe. To notice my body. To hear what I was actually feeling instead of running from it. It's not easy. But it's honest. And honest is where healing starts.

Reflection: What does your body feel like when you're actually in the present? What pulls you out?

_____

_____

_____

_____

_____

_____

Now is the only place your power lives. Not in the past where you bled. Not in the future you fear. But here. In your breath. In your skin. In this choice. So come back. Not because it's comfortable— but because it's real.

My experiences jumping through time involved a psychotic breakdown where I heard voices in my head. Some from the past, some from the future, and not many of them were kind.

But I was dealing with pain, and I spoke to the voices. I gave them names…and now I'm here.

No more voices.

No medications.

Just me—writing a book 15 years later, hoping it helps you find a way through your pain.

.

READY FOR MORE?

Go Deeper: Expanded Reflection Prompts

• Where does your mind go when it drifts—past pain or future panic

---

• What story do you keep reliving that hasn't changed, only deepened?

• What moment are you still trying to rewrite in your head?

• What truth have you avoided facing because it feels stuck in time?

_____

_____

_____

_____

_____

_____

• What anchors you to now—your breath, your body, your truth?

_____

_____

_____

_____

_____

• What does your body feel like when you're not time-traveling?

_____

_____

_____

_____

_____

• What emotion do you run from by escaping into "what if" or "what was"?

_____

_____

_____

_____

_____

_____

• What would healing look like if it didn't depend on an apology or outcome?

_____

_____

_____

_____

_____

• Who taught you that healing had to happen on a deadline?

_____

_____

_____

_____

_____

• What if you stopped rushing and simply started witnessing?

_____

_____

_____

_____

_____

_____

• What belief about time has become a trap for your growth?

_____

_____

_____

_____

_____

• What kind of healing could unfold if you moved at your soul's pace?

_____

_____

_____

_____

_____

• What can you do today that honors your future self—
not just escapes your past?

_____

_____

_____

_____

_____

_____

• What part of you has always known the present is
enough?

_____

_____

_____

_____

_____

• What does your voice sound like when it's not echoing
regret or rehearsing fear?

_____

_____

_____

_____

_____

• How would your life change if you treated this moment like a sacred appointment?

_____

_____

_____

_____

_____

_____

NOT EVERYONE DESERVES ACCESS

If love requires self abandonment,
it's not love.

I used to think love meant sacrificing myself. Bending. Folding. Shrinking. To fit someone else's need. To keep the peace. To feel wanted.

But that wasn't love. That was survival disguised as romance.

They didn't ask me to show up fully. They asked me to show up how they needed me to be.

And I did.

Because I didn't think I had a right to ask for more. For tenderness. For safety. For actual reciprocity.

I called it loyalty. But it was self-abandonment with a smile.

"If being loved means losing yourself, you're not in love —you're in danger."

I've proposed to people emotionally—while they were slapping me with silence, manipulation, and neglect.

And I held the ring out anyway. Begging shadows to accept my light.

It took me years to realize the version of me they wanted wasn't real. And the version that was real? They couldn't sit with him.

Reflection: Who have you loved that couldn't see the real you? Why did you stay?

_____

_____

_____

_____

_____

_____

Love isn't supposed to feel like war. It's not supposed to make you question your worth. Or monitor every word. Or earn basic human kindness.

But when you grow up without healthy love you mistake pain for passion. You mistake anxiety for chemistry. You mistake control for safety.

I've had to unlearn all of that.

That "ride or die" love? It'll take you straight to hell—if you don't check who's driving.

"You don't have to prove you're lovable. You already are."

These days, I love differently. I ask different questions. I pay attention to how people respond when I say no.

Because boundaries don't scare the right people. They only scare the ones who were planning to benefit from your lack of them.

Reflection: What part of yourself do you keep hiding just to keep someone else comfortable?

_____

_____

_____

_____

_____

_____

Not everyone deserves access to you. Not everyone deserves your softness. Not everyone should be handed the map to your soul.

Just because someone wants to be close doesn't mean they deserve proximity to your heart.

They have to respect it. Protect it. Meet you where you are—not where they wish you would shrink to.

And you?

You don't have to kneel for love that hits.

You don't have to chase ghosts hoping they'll feel your light.

You don't have to give anyone the key to your peace unless they know how to hold it gently.

If you played small or gave your heart away —knowing it compromised your integrity— I want you to know you're not alone.

I've done it too. Too often.

What I've learned, doing the work you're doing now, is this:

Real "ride or die" love doesn't ask you to shrink.

It asks you to grow—together.

READY FOR MORE?

Go Deeper: Expanded Reflection Prompts

• What did you call loyalty that was really you disappearing?

_____

_____

_____

_____

_____

_____

• What version of you did someone only love when you stayed small?

_____

_____

_____

_____

_____

• What did you give away just to be chosen?

_____

_____

_____

_____

_____

• How long have you mistaken absence for depth?

_____

_____

_____

_____

_____

• What does your body feel when someone violates your peace?

_____

_____

_____

_____

_____

• What boundary did you set too late—but are still proud of?

_____

_____

_____

_____

_____

• How do you respond when someone asks for access they haven't earned?

_____

_____

_____

_____

_____

_____

• What fear rises when you say "no"?

_____

_____

_____

_____

_____

• What belief about love no longer serves you?

_____

_____

_____

_____

_____

• Where did you learn that love equals pain or chaos?

_____

_____

_____

_____

_____

• What habits still reflect old survival patterns?

_____

_____

_____

_____

_____

• What kind of love are you building now that feels like a return home?

_____

_____

_____

_____

_____

_____

• What part of yourself are you no longer giving away for free?

_____

_____

_____

_____

_____

_____

• What does it mean to give someone a "key" to your peace?

_____

_____

_____

_____

_____

_____

• Who in your life respects your boundaries without testing them?

_____

_____

_____

_____

_____

_____

• What does real safety feel like in a relationship with another person?

_____

_____

_____

_____

_____

_____

DON'T CALL IT LOVE IF YOU'RE STARVING

Fear will do a damn good impression of love.

We don't always act from love. We act from hunger. From fear. From a desperation to not be left, to not be abandoned, to not feel like we're nothing.

And then we wrap that in nice words. We call it caring. We call it being "all in." We call it love.

But it's not.

It's what happens when love is tied to survival. When you've learned that to be wanted, you have to overextend. Overgive. Overperform. And shrink yourself until you fit into someone else's emptiness.

That's not love. That's starvation. And it's slow death dressed as devotion.

"Fear will do a damn good impression of love— but it'll never feel safe."

I used to chase people I should've walked away from. I used to say "I love you" and mean "Please don't leave me." I used to call control and chaos "passion."

But that wasn't love. That was fear—begging to be held.

Reflection: Who have you tried to save just so you wouldn't feel abandoned? .

_____

_____

_____

_____

_____

_____

Love doesn't beg. It doesn't contort. It doesn't scream over silence trying to be heard.

If your love feels like panic, like overthinking, like disappearing into someone else... It's not love. It's a trauma reenactment.

We're taught to earn love. Perform for it. Compete for it. Bleed for it.

But real love? It just is. It doesn't need you to disappear to be received.

"You can't be loved for who you are while being praised for who you're pretending to be."

I don't want to give love just to feel worthy. I don't want to pour into people who only hold me when it's convenient. I don't want to chase ghosts and call it loyalty.

I want truth. Peace. Reciprocity.

But to get that, I had to stop calling my panic love.

Reflection: What part of you still believes you need to be in pain to feel close to someone?

_____

_____

_____

_____

_____

Love without peace isn't love. It's fear in a costume.

You don't have to keep choosing people who keep you in survival mode.

You don't have to keep handing out your light to people who can't hold it.

You don't have to starve to be fed.

I've given up my peace to appease another person's sense of worth—and in the process, lost my own.

Giving yourself up like that is more than self-sacrifice. It's self-erasure.

It's another mask: the one that says "this pain is normal," "this silence is love."

It's the lie you tell yourself to make the emptiness feel earned.

But that's not love. That's self-degradation at its finest.

READY FOR MORE?

Go Deeper: Expanded Reflection Prompts

• What did you call love that was really a plea not to be abandoned?

_____

_____

_____

_____

_____

_____

• When did overgiving become your way of being chosen?

_____

_____

_____

_____

_____

_____

• What part of you still believes love must be earned through pain?

_____

_____

_____

_____

_____

_____

• Who did you stay with to avoid feeling alone—not because it was love?

_____

_____

_____

_____

_____

• When have you confused chaos with passion?

_____

_____

_____

_____

_____

_____

• What part of you believes you have to fix people to be loved?

_____

_____

_____

_____

_____

_____

• How has fear shaped the way you give or receive affection?

_____

_____

_____

_____

_____

_____

• What does control look like when you're afraid of being left?

_____

_____

_____

_____

_____

_____

• What part of you disappears in relationships—and why?

_____

_____

_____

_____

_____

_____

• What would it mean to stop shrinking to fit someone else's needs?

_____

_____

_____

_____

_____

_____

• What does real love feel like when you imagine being fully seen?

_____

_____

_____

_____

_____

_____

• What's the difference between performing for love
and simply being loved?

_____

_____

_____

_____

_____

_____

• What does emotional starvation look like in your story?

_____

_____

_____

_____

_____

_____

• Who have you poured into that couldn't pour back?

_____

_____

_____

_____

_____

_____

• What would it feel like to choose love that
doesn't demand your disappearance?

_____

_____

_____

_____

_____

_____

• How do you reclaim your worth when someone
won't hold your light?

_____

_____

_____

_____

_____

_____

IF IT COSTS YOU PEACE, IT'S TOO EXPENSIVE

Sometimes abundance is what's waiting on the other side of letting go.

I once worked the graveyard shift at a mental health facility for far too long.

I gave it everything—came in early, stayed late, filled the gaps when others walked out.

The staff turnover was atrocious, but I stayed nearly three years. In that time, I created a new system for client record-keeping—one they eventually adopted as standard practice.

Meanwhile, I was undervalued. Passed over for promotions. Replaced by people who knew the right people, not the right work. I was overworked to the edge of legality—no lunch breaks, no support, handling night shifts alone in a residential facility. I was drained. Mentally. Physically. Financially.

And then—just silence. A false rumor. No questions. No investigation. Just let go.

It led to a lawsuit. One I won. And strangely, it led to something more important: peace.

That break—that loss—was the turning point. It gave me a life that finally feels like mine. The most peace-filled years I've known.

We hold on too long. To jobs. To people. To old versions of ourselves.

Not because we love them, but because we're scared of what happens if we let go.

Scared of failure. Of regret. Of not finding anything better.

So we endure. We convince ourselves it's worth it. That this is just how it's supposed to be.

But deep down, we feel the cost.

The quiet ache. The tight chest. The nights we collapse, not from effort—but from emptiness.

"If it costs you peace, it's too expensive."

Work that drains you. People who only love the version of you that performs. Habits that burn your energy but feed your fear.

We call it loyalty. But loyalty without boundaries is a prison.

Abundance doesn't always feel like more. Sometimes it's a soft no. A walk-away. A better yes waiting on the other side of goodbye.

Reflection: What are you holding onto that no longer feeds you? What fear keeps you in it?

_____

_____

_____

_____

_____

_____

It's hard to leave what you once prayed for. It's hard to walk away from what you once needed to survive.

But you've grown. And sometimes growth means outgrowing what once fit.

You're not betraying your past. You're choosing your future.

Letting go isn't weakness. It's wisdom.

"Sometimes abundance is what's waiting on the other side of letting go."

You don't have to burn out to be worthy.

You don't have to tolerate what hurts you just because it used to help you.

You're allowed to say: this is no longer mine to carry.

Reflection: What's one boundary you need to set—to protect your peace, not your ego?

_____

_____

_____

_____

_____

_____

Peace isn't passive. It's power. And anything that costs it is asking too much.

I used to think that walking away—from jobs, habits, people—meant I was weak.
I'd sit in silence, stewing over what I'd allowed. What others did in my presence. What didn't align with who I said I was. I stayed loyal to things I'd outgrown— because I thought letting go meant giving up.
But now I know two things:

1. No one can treat you worse than you treat yourself.

2. Walking away isn't failure. It's victory. Because at that moment, you're choosing peace. And you're the only one who can make that choice for you.

READY FOR MORE?

Go Deeper: Expanded Reflection Prompts

• What have you stayed loyal to that stopped serving
your growth?

_____

_____

_____

_____

_____

_____

• Where has endurance become a substitute for peace?

_____

_____

_____

_____

_____

_____

• What version of yourself are you protecting that no longer feels true?

_____

_____

_____

_____

_____

_____

• What are you afraid will happen if you finally let go?•

_____

_____

_____

_____

_____

What boundary would honor your peace, not just protect

your pride?

_____

_____

_____

_____

_____

_____

• How do you know the difference between protecting yourself and punishing others?

_____

_____

_____

_____

_____

_____

• What does peace feel like in your body, and when did you last feel it?

_____

_____

_____

_____

_____

_____

• Who teaches you that love still exists when you say no?

_____

_____

_____

_____

_____

_____

• What burden have you carried so long it now feels
like your identity?

_____

_____

_____

_____

_____

_____

• Who taught you that burnout equals worth?

_____

_____

_____

_____

_____

_____

• What part of your peace are you trading for someone
else's comfort?

_____

_____

_____

_____

_____

_____

• What do you fear you'll lose if you put yourself first?

_____

_____

_____

_____

_____

_____

• What are you ready to release that you once fought to keep?

_____

_____

_____

_____

_____

_____

• What relationship, habit, or role no longer fits who you're becoming?

_____

_____

_____

_____

_____

_____

• What would letting go sound like if it was an act of compassion, not failure?

_____

_____

_____

_____

_____

_____

• What future version of you is waiting on the other side of goodbye?

_____

_____

_____

_____

_____

_____

PART III

THE BECOMING

AFTER THE MIRROR

This is where the voice begins to feel like yours.

Not because you finally fixed yourself.
But because you stopped needing to be fixed.

You've stared down the mirror.
You've told the truth out loud.
You've grieved the cost of
silence.
And now—here you are.

Still standing.
Still cracked.
Still whole.

This part of the book isn't about becoming perfect.
It's about becoming honest.

It's the part where you realize power
isn't performance.
Peace isn't passive.
And self-love isn't always soft.

There was a man I met in my years of homelessness that said to me, "I hate who I see in the mirror so I shave in the dark."

There was a time I couldn't meet my own eyes in the mirror, and his words echoed in my head Not because I didn't recognize myself—but because I did. I had finally understood what he meant. The person I saw in the mirror was not the person i knew myself to be or who I wanted to see so I too stopped looking in the mirror.

We spend our lives avoiding the truth we already know.

We stay in situations long after they've expired. We defend relationships that deplete us. We perform roles that hollow us out. We lie to ourselves—and call it strength.

But the mirror doesn't lie. It may be quiet, but it's never wrong.

It's the silence that stings. The reflection that reveals what we tried so hard not to see.

And when we finally stop running, stop numbing, stop spinning our stories... we're left with one thing:

Ourselves.

Raw. Honest. Present.

And for the first time, we see what's been waiting to be seen.

The mirror isn't your enemy. It's your witness.

It doesn't want perfection. It wants presence.

It wants you.

It's the part where your voice comes back home— not as a whisper, but as a knowing.

This is the becoming. Not a transformation.

A return.

Reflection: What's one truth you've been avoiding because you know it would require change?

_____

_____

_____

_____

_____

_____

There's a moment—quiet and heavy—where you can't unsee it.

The pattern. The pain. The part you played.

And in that moment, everything shifts.

Not because the truth changed. But because you finally let it in.

Reflection: What truth are you ready to let in, even if it hurts?

_____

_____

_____

_____

_____

_____

It's not the truth that wounds you—it's the fight against it.

Stillness is where the shift begins.

Where avoidance ends and transformation starts.

Where what was buried comes back to life.

You weren't broken. Just buried.

And you've always been the one with the shovel.

The real betrayal is when you keep lying to yourself about what you see.

But today, you don't have to.

You can look. You can name it. You can meet it.

And you can begin again.

Take a moment. Look at yourself
through the mirrored lens.
Do you like what you see?
Yes? No? Then something needs to
shift. Because either way—you're seeing
the realest version of you hiding in that
reflection.
The one behind the masks. The fog.
The brokenness.
The one you know you are—or who
you know you could be.

The next step is becoming them.

READY FOR MORE?

Go Deeper: Expanded Reflection Prompt

• What truth about your situation have you known—
but been unwilling to face?

_____

_____

_____

_____

_____

_____

• What's the cost of continuing to ignore what you see
clearly?

_____

_____

_____

_____

_____

_____

• What lies have you told yourself to avoid being alone?

_____

_____

_____

_____

_____

_____

• When did you first learn to override your own knowing?

_____

_____

_____

_____

_____

_____

• What version of you does your reflection keep trying to return you to?

_____

_____

_____

_____

_____

_____

• What emotion rises when you stop deflecting and just listen?

_____

_____

_____

_____

_____

_____

• What part of yourself have you buried to make others comfortable?

_____

_____

_____

_____

_____

_____

• What part of your identity is a performance built to survive?

_____

_____

_____

_____

_____

_____

• What truth are you ready to say out loud—even if no one else is ready to hear it?

_____

_____

_____

_____

_____

_____

• What belief needs to be released so you can finally see yourself clearly?

_____

_____

_____

_____

_____

_____

• Who do you become when you're not shape-shifting to be loved?

_____

_____

_____

_____

_____

_____

• What fear shows up when you're fully honest with yourself ?

_____
_____
_____
_____
_____
_____

• What grief have you avoided because it would unravel too much?

_____
_____
_____
_____
_____
_____

• What would it feel like to meet your own eyes—and not flinch?

_____
_____
_____
_____
_____
_____

• What becomes possible when you stop lying to yourself ?

_____

_____

_____

_____

_____

_____

• What does your truth sound like—when it isn't afraid?

_____

_____

_____

_____

_____

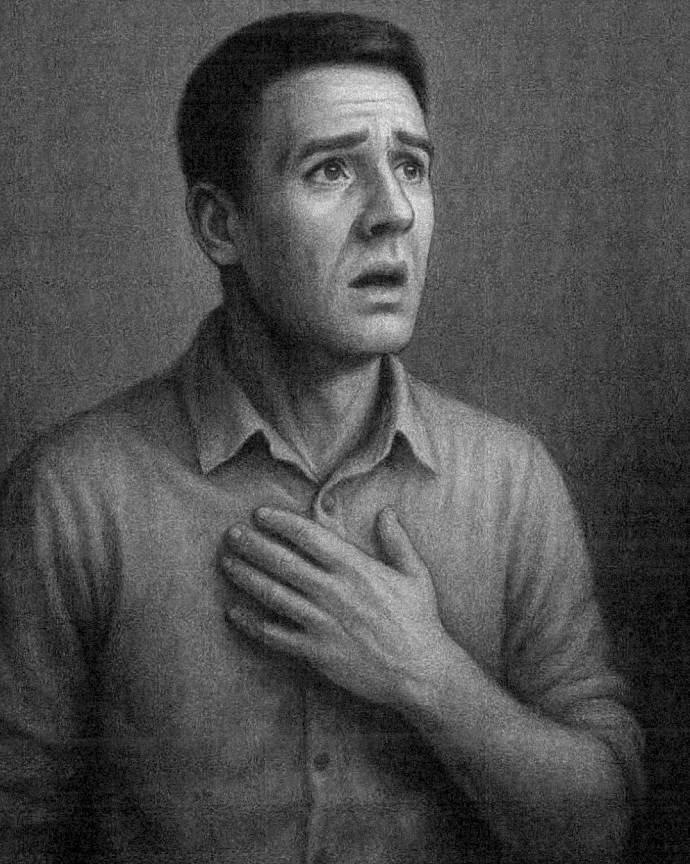

The moment the voice in your head becomes your own and one you recognize isn't some prolific mind altering experience its the culmination of many small moments that laser in on what you've been trying to do the entire time. Ya, you may have some heavy specific ones, like the day I Chose to stay in a child's life even though he isnt mine because he deserves a real father not the version he'd have to imagine in his head, or the moment you forgive those who wronged you. But especially the moment you take the mask off in the mirror and realize the mask, the face, and the voice are all becoming one.. Becoming you.

There comes a moment—not loud, not grand—where the seeking stops. Not because you gave up, but because something clicks. Quietly.

Like the sound of your own name finally said in your own voice.

At first, you might not trust it.

You'll wonder: Is this clarity? Or just another passing thought?

But there's a weight to it. A groundedness. It doesn't try to convince you.

It just is.

You've spent so long chasing peace, wholeness, closure—

All while missing the fact that a voice was guiding you back the whole time.

It wasn't a new voice.

It was yours—beneath the noise, beneath the fear, beneath every mask you thought you had to wear to be loved.

161

Reflection: When did you first notice your inner voice shifting?

_____

_____

_____

_____

_____

_____

This voice didn't yell.

It didn't demand.

It waited.

Patient. Quiet.

Speaking in instinct, in resistance, in goosebumps.

It showed up in your No. In your Not this time. In your I'm tired of pretending.

Reflection: What does that voice sound like now? What does it say?

_____

_____

_____

_____

_____

_____

Maybe the voice has been with you since the beginning.

Maybe it got drowned out by shame, or guilt, or a need to please.

But here's the truth:

You're not broken.

You're not behind.

You're just home

now. And this voice?

It's not mystical. It's not magical. It's just yours.

And it always was.

Reflection: What's the first honest thing you need to say to yourself —out loud?

_____

_____

_____

_____

_____

_____

If you've made it this far, you should be proud
of yourself.
There's one last set of reflections waiting—for your
becoming.

And if you've found even a part of this book valuable,
I urge you to pass it on.
Because the way you moved through these pages?
That's how I survived my life.
In pieces.
In chapters.

From a fractured childhood...
to a disrupted adolescence...
to a chaotic early adulthood...
to a full psychotic breakdown.

And now—here in my thirties.
No therapy. No meds.
Just introspection.
Just reflection.
Drawing lines from A to B to figure out why I am
the way I am—
and how to become better.

Better than the ones before me.
Better than I was yesterday..

READY FOR MORE?

Go Deeper: Expanded Reflection Prompts

• When did you start trusting your own instincts again?

_____

_____

_____

_____

_____

_____

• What words feel like you now?

_____

_____

_____

_____

_____

• What old beliefs no longer sound true in your head?

_____

_____

_____

_____

_____

_____

• What's one moment you heard yourself clearly, and listened?

_____

_____

_____

_____

_____

_____

• When have you silenced yourself to be accepted?

_____

_____

_____

_____

_____

• What truth are you finally ready to speak?

_____

_____

_____

_____

_____

_____

• What does your empowered voice feel like in your body?

_____

_____

_____

_____

_____

• When do you ignore your voice—and why?

_____

_____

_____

_____

_____

• What relationships change when you speak from your truth?

_____

_____

_____

_____

_____

• What's one thing your voice told you that saved you?

_____

_____

_____

_____

_____

_____

• When have you been louder for others than for yourself?

_____

_____

_____

_____

_____

_____

• What part of your voice is still afraid to be heard?

_____

_____

_____

_____

_____

_____

• What version of you is speaking now?

_____

_____

_____

_____

_____

• What do you no longer need to say out loud to believe?

_____

_____

_____

_____

_____

• How will you protect your voice from now on?

_____

_____

_____

_____

_____

AFTERWORD – YOU KNOW A WRAITH

There's no final chapter to healing.

Only pauses.

Only moments where you look back and realize…

you didn't disappear. You became.

This book was never about me.

It was about the parts of you you've been trying to
meet in silence.

The voice you buried.

The mask you wore so long it forgot your face.

You made it here—not because you had all
the answers,

but because you were finally willing to ask
better questions.

That's what this is.

Not a lesson. Not a fix. Not a formula.

A mirror.

A reckoning.

A reclamation.

And if anything in these pages felt like it came from inside you—

it's because it did.

You may not know my name.

You will know me as Noah Wraith.

And I chose this name because I believe we all know a wraith—

A ghost. A shadow. A presence that lingers behind our eyes.

Something we carry. Something we fear.

Something we learn to face.

And I think if you ever truly knew its name—

you would know a Wraith.

SO WHO ARE YOU REALLY?

This section is about a reclamation of your personal power.

You made it this far—now declare who you are, what you are, and what you want to achieve.

Talk about it in the present tense.

State it as though it already exists.

Start here:

• I am the version of myself I used to think was impossible because...

_____

_____

_____

• I am no longer afraid to speak because...

_____

_____

_____

• I am not what they said I was—I am...

_____

_____

_____

- I am worthy of peace, and I live it when I...

_____

_____

_____

- I am not shrinking anymore—I am expanding through...

_____

_____

_____

- I am the one writing this story, and I say...

_____

_____

_____

- I am not waiting for permission because now I know...

_____

_____

_____

- I am proud to be someone who...

_____

_____

_____

Now write it like you mean it:

Fill this space with truth. Say it like it's already real. No disclaimers. No apologies.

I am

_____

_____

I am

_____

_____

I am

_____

_____

I am

_____

_____

I am

_____

_____

I am

_____

_____

I am

_____

_____

I am

_____

_____

_I am

_____

_____

I am

_____

_____

I am

_____

_____

I am

_____

_____

_I am

_____

_____

I am

_____

_____

Look back on this section when you need a reminder of the work you've done and the work you intend to do. This is your reminder that you are worthy, that you are capable of change.

My last challenge to you is if this book helped you pass the knowledge onto someone else so they too may grow into a better version of themselves. Each person that grows pushes the collective as a whole toward a better life. You went through hell and you've finally come home with a map.

ACKNOWLEDGMENTS

This book wouldn't exist if it hadn't been for every single awful thing that ever happened in my life—

and the same can be said for every brilliant light that found its way into it too.

Mom. Dad.

It's okay. I truly do forgive you.

If I'm being honest, I'm thankful.

Without either of you, this book would not have been possible.

Please—look in the mirror and forgive yourselves.

To my Aunt—

the one who showed me what unconditional love feels like,

who held me together when I was falling apart at the seams,

who loved me through moments I didn't even know I wanted to die—

Thank you for being the reason I held on.

To Mr. Houghton—

my middle school teacher,

the one who let me be part of what I now realize was a
remarkable social experiment in human growth—

thank you for cultivating something in me that no one else saw.

To my Best Friends—

my brothers.

You were my anchors growing up.

I'm proud of the men you've become. I carry you both with me.

To my Son—

you may not be mine by blood, but you carry my soul in
everything you do.

I'm beyond proud of the boy you are, and the man I
know you'll be.

You've taught me how to be a man in ways I never expected.

Thank you.

To those I did wrong, and those who wronged me:
I'm sorry.

I forgive you.

Please forgive me.

And most of all—please forgive yourselves.

To those who aren't here to see this become real:
I miss you.

You are etched into every line of this story.

Your fingerprints are on my soul, and they're not
going anywhere.

And to the dog who saved me from myself—Kano.

You were the best girl.

I wish I'd known you were sick.

You sent me the karma I

needed.

You gave me the push to begin this book.

You were, and always will be, my good luck charm.

From 940 to 949—

Change is inevitable.

Just make sure it's for the best.

Thank you. All of you.

The Loop-breaker Soundtrack

These are the songs that saw me when I didn't know
how to speak.
When the voice in my head was too loud to quiet,
these tracks became mirrors, anchors, gut punches.
Some reminded me of what I lost.
Others reminded me I was still here.
I'm not saying they'll save you.
But they might meet you in the same dark and
remind you—you're not alone in it.

Staind – It's Been Awhile
The apology I never said out loud. This one still hits.

3 Doors Down – Kryptonite
The version of me that kept breaking but still tried to save everyone.

Linkin Park – Leave Out All the Rest
The Song I want played at my funeral when I die. Remember me for
the good I did not the pain I had or caused.

Simple Plan – Perfect
The father wound. The ache. The unspoken need.

Seether – Broken (ft. Amy Lee)
When love hurt more than it healed—but I still clung to the echo.

Jelly Roll – Creature

Is it a monster, is it a friend, am I really as bad as I believe.

Smile Empty Soul – Silhouettes

I will find a way to be better than my parents. I won't fill my kids with
brokenness.

Audioslave – Like a Stone

I contemplated my own demise often to the tune of this song and others.

Colbie Caillat – Realize

This song brought me back often to a simpler more loving time in my life.

Sick Puppies – All the Same

This song gave me hope that the ones who left would eventually come back even if they were filled with scars.

Fort Minor – Remember The Name

This Song pushed me to continue my journey more times than I can count.

Kenny Rogers – Coward of the County

This song wasn't chosen by me but I was told it represented me growing up, a father in prison a kind soul and a rage inside that came out when I saw the ones I loved being hurt.

Atmosphere – Always Coming Back Home to You

This song became my compass during my mental breakdown it helped me constantly come back to center.

Immortal Technique (ft. Jean Grea) – You Never Know

This song taught me a lot about love and how fragile it can really be.

Kansas – Carry on My Wayward Son

The fandom I follow aside, it reminds me of both myself and my dad. An emotional hit when you find the right space.

Marshmello – Happier

Particularly the video after my dog passed away this song was my home for weeks

If this book cracked something open, good.
It was never meant to leave you clean—

it was meant to leave you *honest.*
The work doesn't end here. It just goes deeper.
And you don't have to do it alone.

We're building a tribe of Loopbreakers.
People who are done performing peace.
People who are choosing to live with their eyes open—

even when it costs everything.

I'm not offering a brand.
I'm offering a mirror, a drumbeat, and a place to walk
alongside others doing the same.

You'll find me here:

IG @im_the_voice_in_your_head_
Facebook: *The Voice in Your
Head* TikTok:
@voice_in_your_head_

Come as you are.
Stay if it's true.
Bring your voice.

I truly appreciate you.

Rest well Loopreaker

you've earned it.

-Noah

You've just heard the Voice in Your Head.